NLP

Methods For Exerting Influence On Individuals Via Manipulative Techniques Of Mental Control, Hypnotism, And Persuasion

(The Importance Of Acquiring Profound Knowledge In The Covert NLP Strategies For Comprehending)

Hinrich Weise

TABLE OF CONTNET

Tools For Successfully Reprogramming Your Unconscious Mind 1

ADVANCES IN INTERPERSONAL COMMUNICATION: 9

Nlp Methods 21

Using Npl To Control Thoughts 31

Simple Techniques Manipulators Employ 55

Revealing The Shadowy Convictor 72

Establishing And Changing Patterns 97

Dark Psychology: Who Uses It To Impact People? 118

Tools For Successfully Reprogramming Your Unconscious Mind

The portion of your experiences and sensations you are ignorant of is your unconscious mind. One's health and recovery account for a significant portion of the conscious phase of life. It is important to remember that many people interpret physical or mental symptoms as responses or reactions that, for the most part, happen at the unconscious level in people. Thus, the brain's automatic functions comprise the unconscious aspect of the soul. It is important to realize that memories are involved in these processes. As a result, the unconscious mind is essential for retaining all of the memories and events that are not being actively thought about. Additionally, these sections contain a variety of concerns that need to be addressed and disturb people's minds.

Here are a few resources to assist you in adopting the proper perspective to change your life:

Develop a Positive Thought Process
Affirmations are a terrific technique to help your brain fire in new ideas and rewire them to believe that you are still healthy. Retraining your brain to believe these things should be one of your main aims. The unconscious does not process negative thoughts. As a result, it is crucial that you, as an individual, start by outlining your ideas and by having some clear objectives. Not only will positive thinking enable you to speak with the unconscious mind, but it will also improve your brain's speed and activity levels. As a result, when you embrace optimism, you continually clear out some of the negative thoughts that arise and revitalize your account.

Your thoughts will typically be more inclined to think clearly and optimistically. You will become more effective in life since your thoughts will have more energy to retain what is required. As a result, try to keep a positive outlook and ensure you are well-absorbed in a lot of optimism. This feature is crucial since it will promote beneficial brain growth and expansion.

Innovative Visualization

Using creative visualization to visualize achievement is indeed effective. Instead of focusing on the processes required to get there, you should focus on the final goals you wish to achieve. The emotions in your pictures will be absorbed by your mind as though they were genuine, giving you the inner assurance you require to bring your dreams to life. Your belief system strengthens, and your mind assists you in figuring out the procedures to turn that vision into reality as you learn to imagine your end goals. When you can communicate and think positively instead of negatively, your account can grasp your intentions and support your objectives. As you keep doing this, you can remove the unfavorable image from your thoughts and embrace more of life's important qualities. It is important to remember that clearing one's mind of questions, anxieties, and other life-related concerns is key to understanding what is truly important. Therefore, developing good life visualizations through mental training is essential for brain growth.

Meditating

You must use reflection to rewire your mentality. Reflection is essential to keep your account focused on your work and prevent setbacks. It is important to remember that while you meditate, you are using the brain's subconscious technique. Everything you think of is thus well captured and preserved. The ability to balance all emotions with the physical side of life makes meditation essential. Another benefit of reflection is that it strengthens one's mental endurance. As a result, you will be able to reflect carefully and develop ideas that will last. You can gain control over your unconscious mind by practicing deep meditation and realizing that your thoughts originate from a neural net passed down to you over several billion years of evolution. This neural net is shaped and transacted by your nested culture and environment and by the lessons you have learned and retained. You must instill in your mind the importance of meditation. This feature lets your brain let go of negative life experiences and concentrate on your accomplishments. One can identify the easily created aspects of life during meditation. An individual gains more experience from the element as a better way of life is cultivated in their thoughts.

Brainstorming and Mind Mapping

During brainstorming aids in issue-solving, mind mapping uses visual representations to illustrate the connections between concepts or facts. You are advised to dedicate at least thirty minutes a day to spout any goals that occur to you, regardless of their relevance; in general, you should begin with a particular subject or program. Before you begin writing what comes into your account, you should take a moment to clear your head and concentrate on that subject. Keep all of those concepts handy for a later review. When your conscious mind connects the dots, the seemingly random notes you generate during a brainstorming session will make sense to you. The earlier brainstorming sessions will spark fresh concepts that will give your account a stronger voice while searching for the solutions you require to support you in realizing your aspirations. Regular practice will yield unexpected insights and opportunities you would not have otherwise had. Seeing what ideas you can come up with when you start writing things down will also be entertaining.

Consciousness

An essential first step is to become interested and aware of your worries and limiting beliefs. You will continue to act as though your ideas and opinions are unquestionable because you are a prisoner to your thoughts and no longer actively questioning their integrity. It's simple to realize how false and even dangerous those thoughts are when you take the time to slow down and examine them. This makes it much simpler to actively choose other thoughts and beliefs to take their place.

Entrance

One human state known as hypnosis entails directing attention toward an increased ability to respond to suggestion and decreased peripheral awareness. Remembering that hypnosis is supposed to enhance concentration and focus on the subject is important. It's also important to remember that the process starts with the induction of anesthesia, which typically entails several initial recommendations and instructions. Thus, the hypnotist speaks to the subject gradually until they are calmer and receptive, which tends to deliver and empower some good ideas into the subject's unconscious mind. It is important to note that you will likely follow the hypnotist's instructions while in this condition and have a tendency to observe, feel, detect, and possibly perceive. The main distinction between guided meditation and hypnosis is that you are choosing the music to play in your mind during the former. When relaxed, your brain is inherently far more receptive to the power of suggestion. You need to use this tendency for your goals to rewire your mind for success.

ADVANCES IN INTERPERSONAL COMMUNICATION:

NLP provides several strategies to help you become a more proficient interpersonal communicator if you aim to improve your communication skills and interpersonal relationships. Among these are methods like "calibration," which opens the door to additional methods like "matching," "mirroring," and "leading and pacing."

To determine if a person's eye-accessing cues align with the majority, all it takes to calibrate is to ask some questions that you know are true of the person you are speaking with (obvious replies, in other words). For instance, when you ask someone what color the sky is when you're inside, they should look up and to the left, remembering that the sky is blue, before responding. This can help determine whether the individual is processing information similarly to others. Additionally, converse with the person and pay attention to the words they use to calibrate the prevailing accessing cue. They are probably primarily "auditory" in their information coding if they use terms like "hear," "listen," or seem irritated by background noises that other people wouldn't find bothersome. They may even repeat what you say or themselves again.

It's time to move on to matching after you fully understand how someone is built to think—that is, how they process and encode information in their brains. When you match someone's representational system, you are matching them. Returning to the auditory person, you should speak to them in a way that best suits their needs by using auditory words (hear, listen, sound, etc.). One method to establish rapport is this. According to NLP, rapport is established when you can read the other person's body language, tone, and language. This enables you to comprehend how people "map" reality or their "model" of the world. Recall that in lesson 1, we discussed one of the NLP tenets: "The map is not the territory." Rather, it represents a person's understanding of the territory, or their model of the world, and the perspective from which they come in terms of their beliefs or presumptions about how things ought to be and are.

It could be advantageous to mismatch someone in some situations. This is merely acting in opposition to them rather than mirroring them. This can be accomplished in its most severe form by "turning your back" on a person, which undermines rapport. You can mismatch them by turning your back on them; they show you your back while you show them your front. Mismatching can be helpful in situations where you don't want to participate in a conversation. When you mismatch the person speaking about a topic, it can help steer the conversation in the direction you want it to go. As with anything, exercise caution and try not to damage the relationship if you can. You never know when you might find that person a valuable resource for both of you.

Another tactic is mirroring, which is identical to matching but for timing. When utilizing body language matching, matching is carried out gradually over time. You might scratch your nose as we are talking, for instance, but I wouldn't want to respond in kind right away because that could mean that I'm imitating you, which would probably cause us to lose our rapport. On the other hand, mirroring is done carefully and simultaneously. You might want to mirror their movement by raising your left hand in response to someone else's right hand raised. I want to stress that you have to exercise caution while mirroring since it could lead to feelings of irritation and mistrust. When used with decency and honesty, it can be a highly effective method of establishing rapport. In reality, I went for a job interview, and the interviewer put his right arm on the armrest and leaned in that direction. I mirrored him by placing my left arm on my armrest and leaning in the same direction. Who knows why I got the job, but I'm sure it didn't hurt that I did. So try it out for yourself and see what benefits you get from mirroring and matching. I believe you'll be astounded by the beneficial outcomes you start experiencing.

Adversity and Evaluation Directed at You

This conduct will differ from some of the other methods we have covered. In those cases, humor served as a shield that allowed the manipulator to say or do anything they wanted before turning the tables on the victim. With this one, the manipulator is simply picking on their victim and abandoning any lighthearted repartee.

The manipulator can keep their victim off-balance and ensure that they, the manipulator, can continue to feel superior by continuously marginalizing, mocking, and dismissing their victim. Using this strategy, the aggressor would intentionally create the idea that there is always something wrong with their victim and that they would never measure up to the manipulator's expectations, no matter how hard they try.

The manipulator intends to draw attention solely to the negative and unpleasant events. When someone gives regular criticism, the victim may disclose some negative things, but the other person will offer suggestions and solutions that the victim can work on. When manipulating, they will only highlight the negative aspects of the situation and never provide any real or constructive solutions, nor do they present the other person with any worthwhile opportunities for assistance. They enjoy saying and doing things meant to hurt the other person.

Applying the Quiet Approach

I think we've all used this one at some point. We will become enraged with someone or believe they have wronged us somehow, in which case we will cut off communication. We believe that by having them work for what we want for a little while, we are increasing our chances of getting what we want and that when we don't offer them our whole attention, we are causing them some suffering.

This is a strategy that many manipulators will employ as well. The manipulator will assume control if they purposefully ignore the victim's reasonable calls, texts, emails, and other correspondence. They are having the victim do all the work, which may cause the other person to feel a little unsure and doubtful. The silent game is mental in which the manipulator can exploit the victim's silence as leverage.

Acting As Though They Don't Know What They're Doing

The next deception you can encounter is "feigning ignorance." Essentially, this is the game of being stupid. The manipulator will force their victim to assume responsibility and may even cause them to sweat if they pretend not to comprehend what the victim desires or would like the manipulator to accomplish.

Examples of this type of action abound in the contemporary world. Occasionally, kids will employ this strategy to put off, postpone, and coerce adults into completing tasks for them that they don't want to undertake, like tidying their rooms. Adults are also capable of employing this kind of strategy. Adults will occasionally engage in this type of conduct or strategy when attempting to conceal information, fulfill a duty, or avoid doing a task.

Feeling of Remorse

The manipulator can use guilt-baiting to exploit the target's emotional frailties and vulnerabilities. This is one way the manipulator might force the victim to yield and comply with very irrational demands and requests. Several instances can occur when attempting to utilize guilt baiting as a kind of manipulation tactic. This could entail making the victim answerable for the manipulator's failures and sadness and the manipulator's success and happiness. Additionally, the manipulator could play on the victims' vulnerabilities by placing irrational blame on them.

Victim-hood

Victimization can take many different forms when it comes from a manipulator. This could involve the actor portraying themselves as the helpless, feeble martyr. They could pretend to be weak on purpose to win the compassion and favor of others around them. In addition to imagined or exaggerated personal difficulties, there are occasionally considered or exaggerated health issues.

This behavior is intended to take advantage of the recipient's kindness. It can also take advantage of the other person's sense of responsibility, obligation, guilt, and nurturing instinct to obtain unjustifiable concessions and benefits that the victim probably wouldn't provide to other individuals who weren't in the same situation.

Contemporary Marketing

Advertising is sometimes perceived as both manipulation and persuasion, but it is often seen as the former. There are many well-known advertisements out there that concentrate on manipulating people to assist them in achieving their goals. They can use foot-in-the-door tactics, demonstrating why other people are interested in the goods and more.

While many of us would prefer to believe that we are too intelligent to be duped by manipulative ads, the internet, and other sources, the truth is that many marketers are getting more skilled at what they do as time goes on. They are meant to persuade you to choose one product over another or buy something you don't need. If they are successful, the business will be able to profit, and you will have to pay your money to purchase the product.

Even though we may believe that advertising cannot influence us, this is untrue. Every time you go to the store, you have at least a slight tendency to choose one product over another based on the commercials you saw. Indeed, you might have chosen it due to its affordability, flavor, or the way it fits you, but previous advertisements influenced at least a portion of your choice.

That manipulation may appear in your daily life. Various manipulations could appear in your life, depending on who you spend time with. When attempting to manipulate someone else, knowing what these are and how to employ them can also help guarantee the desired outcomes.

Nlp Methods

securing

The goal of anchoring is to assist you in altering your mental state. It can assist you in remaining composed in the face of peril or difficulty, as well as in unwinding and acting appropriately when others try to agitate you.

The goal of anchoring is to replicate a Pavlovian experiment. Pavlov rang a bell while the dogs were being fed in one of his canine experiments. The dogs would drool in anticipation of their meals whenever they saw the food and heard the bells. Eventually, Pavlov started ringing the bell without showing the dogs the food, and he saw that the dogs would drool at the sound of the bells regardless of the presence of food.

Anchors work similarly, inducing a mental response that regulates feelings and ideas. Rubbing your forehead, for example, might act as an anchor. Involuntary anchoring might occur occasionally. For example, a familiar scent may evoke memories from your early years, while a song may remind you of your former partner. These are a few instances of involuntary anchors that function without requiring a self-initiated trigger.

Creating stimuli during the resourceful state is the first step in establishing anchors, allowing the resourceful state to link with the anchor. You can create personal anchors that will set off a desired response in you anytime you encounter anything, much like the dogs that start drooling for food even when there isn't any in sight.

Producing the anchor after it has been formed to cause the occurrence of the resourceful state is referred to as "activating the anchor."

You react to certain anchors in your life when you are joyful or depressed. You respond to certain anchors whether or not you are feeling driven and self-assured, even though there are instances when you are unaware of what these anchors are. That's why you could occasionally find yourself in a foul mood without realizing it. Using the NLP anchoring technique, you can create your unique anchors and use them to create the desired state of mind. To induce a calm response in oneself, for example, you can employ known anchors if you are nervous before an interview yet want to appear composed. You can utilize anchors to calm yourself down if someone is bothering you, but you don't want to lose your cool.

Breakdown in Pattern

Consider a scenario in which you have a daily commute from your house to work and travel through your preferred route every time. This driving pattern gets monotonous, and you may not always need to put in as much effort or focus since you already know the drill.

You use this time to reflect on your day, the chores you must finish at home, and other matters while your subconscious takes care of the rest. It works almost like autopilot for you.

All of a sudden, there's a huge noise, then boom! There's a big tree that fell and blocked your way. The automobile screeches to a stop when you apply the brakes forcefully. You sat in your car for a few seconds, not understanding what happened.

Your subconscious does not know how to react because it is not accustomed to this circumstance. This is when you have to intervene; your conscious mind needs to take over and give directives on how to deal with the circumstance. The ability of your subconscious mind to carry out automatic patterns frees up your conscious mind to tackle other tasks that require conscious thought.

Sometimes, automatic behaviors, thoughts, feelings, and actions might cause issues when attempting to change certain patterns. It's not like you're unwilling to change; you keep doing the same thing repeatedly because your subconscious keeps dragging you back.

You must realize that the subconscious mind is not very good at making decisions. Decision-making is limited to the conscious mind. Pattern interruption is an NLP technique that puts your subconscious mind in waiting mode while it gets information from your conscious mind.

It enables you to adopt new behaviors and approaches and overcome old ones. It assists you in reprogramming your subconscious to function as a messenger for the conscious mind, receiving instructions.

The Swish Method

The Swish NLP approach helps you adjust how your memories influence you. It assists you in distancing yourself from strong, unfavorable ideas that give rise to unfavorable emotions that could harm you and your life.

The swish NLP approach can help you control your thoughts and feelings, particularly those that are connected to what is going on in your environment. With this NLP technique, you may detach yourself from past thoughts—such as those that annoyed or embarrassed you in the past—from present-day emotions brought on by self-defeating thoughts and from worries about situations that are coming up or that you may encounter in the future.

For example, if you take a leave of absence from work due to illness or stress and you start to worry about returning to work, this is an unwelcome bad feeling that is a worry in this situation. Your heart races and your stomach churns whenever you realize you must return to work the following week and enter your workplace. This indicates that entering that office serves as the catalyst.

You investigated this sensation to make sure there were any logical causes for your anxiety, but there aren't any, as you verified with your bosses, and everything is fine. You now wish to avoid feeling anxious or scared when entering your workplace the following week. You should approach it with enthusiasm and confidence.

The Swish technique can help you swap out these negative emotions for happiness.

The Framing Technique of NLP

The NLP Framing approach is based on the notion that your perspective affects what you see. Framing is attempting to alter the context or setting of something to alter the meaning you associate with it.

For example, someone trying to irritate you may seem humorous, making you laugh at them instead of getting upset. The way you frame events and things around you determines the significance you give them.

You can alter the meaning by responding and acting in different ways. Even though it's the same costume and the same person wearing it, people would perceive it differently if they dressed like skeletons for a Halloween party and a funeral.

Reframing is a technique used in NLP that helps you view and understand events differently so that you can act differently. By reinterpreting events and communicating differently to elicit a different response, you can persuade individuals to perceive things differently. By employing this strategy, you may remain composed in the face of terror and remain cool when you should be furious or lose your cool.

Reflecting and Establishing Communication
Mirroring is imitating or replicating the mannerisms, demeanor, or speech patterns of the individual you are interacting with.

Remember that mimicking someone is not the same as mirroring them. Copying whatever someone does is called aping; this is impolite and differs from mirroring.

Mirroring has to appear unconscious and be so subtle that the individual whose body language and speech patterns you are trying to copy can hardly notice it.

You can imitate someone to mirror them:

* Vocabulary style or particular word choices * Body language * Speech patterns * Pace, tempo, pitch, tone, and loudness

Mirroring facilitates rapport-building with the other person you are speaking with. It enables the other person to get to know you, trust you, and warm up to you. You can't have a successful interaction unless you and the other person you communicate with continue to get along.

Mirroring can be done in two ways: highlighting the similarities or the distinctions between you and the other person. Stressing the commonalities removes resentment and reluctance.

Mirroring comes naturally to most people. If you are trying to communicate with a small child, for example, you could crouch so that you and the child are at the same height or speak more slowly so that the youngster can hear you and comprehend you better. Here's an illustration of how we automatically mimic other people.

Using Npl To Control Thoughts

NLP, the psyche, and final authority

Have you ever questioned how some people manage change positively and innovatively? Changes in their lives throw some people off balance, yet others fit in just fine. How come certain individuals always seem to be in the right place at the right time? Why can some people maintain healthy relationships while others cannot maintain one for a week? Are some people more successful than others due to some sort of natural ability or luck?

In the 1970s, Richard Bandler, a student of University of California professor John Grinder, began working on a behavioral study project. They studied the habits of the prosperous and were more curious about the reasons behind the exceptional abilities of some people than those of others. The discoveries aided their development of neurolinguistic programming, which involves studying, codifying, and reproducing successful people's actions and cognitive patterns. The connection between our brain (how we think), linguistics (how we communicate), and programs (our patterns of emotions and behaviors) is examined in the programming.

The foundation of neuro-linguistic programming is the idea that successful actions may be replicated. The differences between successful and failed people's mental processes, actions, and linguistic usage piqued the curiosity of both the lecturer and the student. Today's NLP is based on their findings. Simply put, the researchers asserted that luck plays little in success. It is not necessary to be fortunate to succeed. Adapting your life philosophy can help you succeed in various areas, including relationships, work, social interactions, and other circumstances. Even so, certain individuals create innate strategies for success; anyone prepared to put in the effort may master these speaking, acting, and thinking methods.

Although the Neurolinguistics programming was created many years ago, there have been numerous revisions since then. Nowadays, NLP is a widely employed method in therapy and self-improvement. It is employed by the military, industry, education, and, most importantly, individuals. NLP may be effectively used in personal situations, and many large corporations provide their employees with training on how to apply NLP to clients.

NLP studies how our minds create spoken descriptions, sounds, and visuals of various contexts. Understanding our internal reality maps makes it simpler to intentionally alter our inner terrain and, as a result, alter how we react to the people and circumstances in our external environment.

Seeing results immediately is one of the key advantages of using NLP. For example, NLP approaches allow for the treatment of certain phobias in individuals in a matter of minutes. Furthermore, NLP may be used to deal rapidly and efficiently with concerns and barriers. To be honest, NLP has provided great insight into our interactions with our social and physical environments and other facets of life.

Mind control, NLP, and manipulation

Is NLP able to assist you in avoiding mind control and negative manipulation? Indeed, NLP may assist everyone in combating manipulators. We frequently live on complete autopilot, reacting to events mostly on autopilot. As a result, we are more susceptible to manipulation as we seldom exercise critical judgment or analysis. When we go through life automatically, we often follow the example set by others (social proof) and let other people's decisions affect us. Go Sometimes driven by the subconscious scripts we have learned and used for years—some of which we have used since we were young—as we go through life.

It can be difficult for some proponents of personal development and change to explain how to avoid using the particular instruments we should use to better our lives. However, NLP provides the resources you need to make that adjustment. It teaches you that you are accountable for the deeds, emotions, and answers you take to the circumstances in your life. Instead of letting someone else drive you around, NLP enables you to take control of your life and grab the wheel.

NLP is used more frequently because it is practical, various problems may be solved, and its tools are useful. Among the problems are a few of them:

● Building stronger connections,

- Gaining greater health
- Overcoming phobias and anxieties, such as social anxiety

To put it plainly,

- Enhancing correspondence
- Increasing your professional success and influence and

household life.

Excellence is necessary for success in any area of life, including work, sports, family, etc. Neuro-linguistic programming provides a path to this superiority. Most NLP techniques must be used, even though other elements, including natural aptitude and luck, influence success. The foreseeable outcome of thinking and doing in a particular way is a success.

Are you Stoic, Emotional, or Both?

How do you respond at first when faced with a tough choice or tense circumstance? Regardless of how things turn out, your response to unpleasant stimuli can reveal a lot about the architecture of your brain. Even though nobody enjoys receiving bad news, our reactions can indicate useful applications of NLP.

Using an example here:

John has been working on an important customer presentation; he is your teammate. You may be well-versed in the subject but are not as knowledgeable as John. The day before the important meeting, John gets involved in a car accident and sustains some injuries. John will be alright, but you need to seal the deal. He is unable to reschedule due to the clients. How ought one to proceed?

Let's start by examining the adverse stimuli:

John, your friend, suffered harm!

John is a coworker; thus, you need to perform your duties.

You are frustrated because the clients won't let you reschedule your meeting. You might respond emotionally if you feel like you need to stress out, scream, or swear. Any negative inputs would be disregarded, and you would just ignore them if you were a stoic thinker. It is possible to be both. An answer is never right or wrong. Both stoic and emotional thinkers can utilize NLP to set goals and de-stress for the current activity.

The word "modeling" will be used a lot in this text. It is a crucial component of the neurolinguistic programming system. We will delve deeper into mental modeling and visualization with each chapter. NLP cannot be used effectively without a thorough understanding of modeling and how it operates.

This is a really basic illustration. You would want to emulate his actions based on his preparation of the content, his approach to business, and his personality. We can imitate what others do and learn from them.

How Creative Are You?

Imagination is instilled in us from an early age. Children who complain about boredom often hear from their parents, "Go play!" What is imagination? What does imagination mean, and how does NLP use it?

What is the real meaning of this? This suggests that our ability to visualize fictional characters, create mental images, and generate ideas during brainstorming sessions is all a result of our imagination. Imagination serves a cognitive role by enabling us to deliberate before acting.

The foundation of the NLP technique is these cognitive processes. For this reason, having a creative imagination is crucial to practicing NLP successfully. What if you believe your imagination is lacking? Your imagination is limitless, but you might not know how to put it to use. You can learn, even if you're too old to do so!

You may also believe you lack imagination simply because you are unaware of it. Those who think linearly assume they are not imaginative. This is untrue. Just as imaginative as creating botanical gardens or learning to sing is the ability to logically solve complex problems utilizing a sequence of functions. Not everyone has the same capacity for imagination and originality as abstract artists.

Imagination is the foundation of all human endeavors and achievements. Engineers and scientists launched astronauts to the Moon because someone thought it was possible. Without imagination, the human race would not have made the creative and technological advancements that make living in the twenty-first century magnificent. Every day, organ transplants and brain surgeries are carried out all over the world because someone has the guts to ask, "What if?"

If you don't think you have much creativity, you can work on it and exercise it. If you don't use your imagination frequently, it will degenerate.

Consider what-if scenarios and potential outcomes. After that, engage in learning. We can better research the next course of action and ask inquiries as we gain more knowledge.

Toys can be a terrific way to have fun, regardless of age. Bricks & blocks, coloring books, and doodlepads are examples of toys that can help us redirect our ideas. These toys facilitate focused attention to a single job with an open-ended outcome. Your creativity may flow more freely when you have this freedom to express yourself. Brainteasers, logical puzzles, and rebates are excellent methods to spark your creativity.

You can also search the internet for lovely photos worldwide and engage in minor mental exercises like "imaginary vacations." Select a picture and see yourself in it. Which places would you go see? Which meals or activities are you interested in trying? Though it doesn't take much time, this exercise makes you think beyond what you normally do. It may take you to additional resources regarding a nation or its culture. You'll be able to learn more and develop new cerebral pathways as a result.

The more you use your imagination, the more powerful it will become. Imagination is essential to NLP practice regardless of linear, abstract, dynamic, or stoic thinking style. Gaining more knowledge, solving puzzles, or creating scenarios that call for conceptual thought can enhance your imagination.

Going Over NLP Fundamentals

Now that we fundamentally understand NLP let's review them again.

Visualization:

V: A simple, imaginative NLP exercise

This facilitates your ability to see what you want to see. It takes advantage of internal

Speech to motivate and spark novel actions:

- An elementary NLP technique based on observation

It teaches you how to perceive the world from other people's perspective.

- Promotes effective actions

If you keep practicing modeling and visualizing, you will improve. We'll build on these principles and investigate how NLP might enhance your relationships, communication abilities, and self-concept.

Gaining awareness of and improving your self-concept

Let's talk about beliefs now. They constitute yet another crucial foundational idea in neuro-linguistic programming. Your view of the world and, more significantly, your view of yourself are greatly influenced by your beliefs and values. First, let's review the fundamentals of belief.

NLP.

What Constitutes a Belief?

Everyone will respond to this hard question differently. It's a personal matter that impacts every facet of our existence. Beliefs are the cornerstone of our worldviews, whether simple or sophisticated.

When you consider beliefs, your mind naturally turns to politics and religion. There is much more to belief than this. Believers look in the mirror first thing in the morning. Have faith in the individuals you live with. You have belief in yourself at all times, throughout the day.

For you, what does belief mean? Can one identify who they are based just on their beliefs? How can you recognize your beliefs when you don't know where to look? Are you sure about your beliefs? What actions may you take to alter your beliefs?

We shall be addressing these queries in this chapter. Our main goals will be helping you define your views and who you are. We'll also learn how to use NLP to modify how we see ourselves. Now, let's get going!

Using Neuro-Linguistic Programming (NLP): A Guide

Positive language is the most fundamental principle of NLP. No, I'm not saying that you can ignore all of your difficulties by maintaining a stiff upper lip; rather, this strategy is supported by science. You see, the brain cannot process negative words. This implies that if you say to your communicative partner, "Please do not touch me," they would actually hear in their subconscious, "Please do touch me."

According to NLP, your subconscious mind controls everything, including respiration and digestion. This implies you can also use this method to speak with your subconscious. The theory is that your subconscious would only hear and react to "Do get well" if you were to repeat "Do not get well" to yourself as a mantra. Naturally, it's ideal to employ this kind of negative language on other people rather than on oneself since you can easily just keep repeating mantras that are positive to yourself. The subconscious mind cannot hear negative speech, like "no" or "can't," making it even easier to subtly ingrain ideas into people's subconscious minds without them realizing you are pushing them to act a certain way. This is something that many people are unaware of.

The only period during which you have to be careful of your internal conversation while evaluating the effect of negative language on the subconscious mind is when your self-talk begins employing negatives without your awareness. It is crucial to be aware of the tone of your internal dialogue and to phrase thoughts positively, such as "I hope I am calm during the interview," to avoid a negative speech impact on your brain. For instance, if you accidentally think, "I hope I don't get nervous during this interview," your subconscious mind will hear, "I hope I do get nervous during this interview."

Targeted speaking is the second most important premise in NLP application. According to NLP theory, people can communicate in three main ways: kinesthetic, visual, or aural. Moreover, NLP requires its users to recognize these different communication styles and attempt to determine which one best fits their communicative partner. Introducing new concepts into someone's thinking is considerably simpler when your language matches your distinct communication style.

Listening to someone talk is the greatest approach to determining their communication style. Someone with an auditory style can say things like, "That sounds great," or "I hear you're busy working on a project." Sayings like "This homework is hard," "I feel like you are not listening to me," or even "I'm going through a rough time" are examples of kinesthetic communicators. Conversely, visually communicating people utilize expressions like "Look on the bright side" or "I see you went to the shops again this morning."

Once you've identified the communication partner's preferred style, you can begin using this. When you use gestures and grins to communicate with visual people, you risk them becoming complacent. Another excellent tip is using vivid, detailed language to vividly represent any real locations or objects. This is smart if you want to engage your conversational partner and maintain eye contact.

Auditory learners pay attention to the intonation and tone of a speech. Therefore, it's critical to maintain control over the pitch and tone of your voice, utilizing subtle variations and inflections to keep your conversation partner interested.

Rather than being "thinkers," kinesthetic learners are "feelers." You'll have greater luck communicating with them if you can capitalize on this using expressive language rather than just giving them the facts. Furthermore, because this is the level at which they function, telling them, "I have a gut feeling about this," may increase the likelihood that they will believe you.

It may take some time to discover your communicative partner's communication style because you must first establish a rapport with them. Fortunately, a workaround for this works almost as well as listening to someone's speech habits. It's all about how you observe their eyes.

While speaking, kinesthetic thinkers typically look down, auditory thinkers laterally to the left or right, and visual thinkers up and straight ahead. Observing an individual's eye movements can provide a wealth of information about their preferred communication style and the most effective ways to interact with them.

Mirroring is the next NLP technique, and it's really easy to apply and effective. The mirroring approach is predicated on the notion that people with similar mannerisms and speech patterns are more likely to be trusted. This implies that one might be able to absorb some traits from another person by closely observing them. They will ultimately trust you and see things your way if you do this.

The secret to mirroring is to blend it in as much as possible. Your communicative partner will quickly grow suspicious and question what you are up to if you just mimic their actions. The most effective method of mimicking someone is subtly mimicking their speech patterns. For example, using slang in your discussions with someone who frequently uses it in speech could be a good idea. Not everything can be replicated, though, including speech. An excellent place to start is with gestures. For instance, you might wish to cross your legs if your communication partner sits with them crossed. You'll also need to use some discretion in this situation and avoid copying their every move.

Another NLP technique that practitioners frequently employ is disassociation. Disassociation is typically utilized to assist the individual in overcoming bad feelings rather than on a communicative partner. The stages of using disassociation are as follows:

Determine your feelings. Do you feel depressed? Furious?Angry?Maybe afraid?

After pinpointing your sensation, picture yourself leaving your body floating out of your head. Picture yourself gazing down at your body, observing its surroundings and how it responds to the unfavorable feeling you want to get rid of.

Finally, picture a shift in how you feel about yourself. Maybe you feel a knot in your chest constricting from anxiety; now, picture that knot slowly unfurling and becoming loose and relaxed.

The next approach is anchoring, which can also be applied to communicative partners. Anchoring came from Ivan Pavlov's idea of classical conditioning. Pavlov experimented by ringing a bell each time his dogs finished eating. After a while, Pavlov convinced the dogs to salivate only by ringing the bell, even when there was no food. In many ways, anchoring functions similarly.

Begin by training a conversational partner with a certain gesture or word before employing anchoring on them. Use this gesture or word to connect these two experiences in your communication partner's mind whenever they're feeling the emotion you want to evoke in the future. If you have successfully established an "anchor," you ought to be able to evoke this feeling in your communicative partner just by uttering the word or making the gesture in front of them, devoid of any outside cues or manipulation.

"Concealed commands" is the name of another really helpful strategy. Asking a question in a way that keeps your communicating partner from realizing that you are pushing them toward a certain result is known as a disguised command. A discreet command could be something like, "Which movie would you want to watch?" rather than enquiring, "Want to watch a movie?"

Because they both largely rely on wordplay, the "if you want" and "concealed commands" techniques are somewhat similar. The "if you want" strategy persuades your conversational partner to do something against your wishes. For instance, if you ask your communication partner, "I can pay the bill if you want," they will assume that since you have already volunteered to do so, politeness requires them to extend the same offer, which you will accept, of course. By doing this, you effectively absolve yourself of any accountability for the issue and place it on your communication partner.

Nevertheless, NLP wordplay extends beyond implicit instructions and the "if you want" tactic. According to NLP, the word "but" is particularly significant because the human mind typically only hears and concentrates on the portion of a sentence that comes after it. For instance, if I were to say, "Susan is a pretty girl, but she has horrible teeth," all my communicative partner would understand would be that Susan has terrible teeth. My communicative partner's thinking would only process that Susan is gorgeous if I rephrased the query to something like, "Susan has horrible teeth, but she is a pretty girl."

Simple Techniques Manipulators Employ

You will begin to reveal more about who you are and what a manipulator is capable of as soon as you understand how awareness of some self-awareness facts can help you identify deceptive behavior in others. Remember, you need to be cautious of the fundamental strategies manipulators employ if you want to defeat them. When clear about what you want and don't want, you may confront a manipulator head-on and even negate some of their common strategies. However, never forget that the trickster loses when you recognize that you are being duped. It all comes down to your will to take the opposite role and transform into the manipulator.

Accusing your opponent of the things he is making you seem bad for

This is commonly known as the act of pointing out the transgressions of another individual.

When they are attacked and find it hard to protect themselves, manipulators usually turn the tables. They accuse their opponent of doing the same crimes for which they are held accountable. "You state that I don't love you! I think it is you who does not cherish me!"

Making a Power Appeal

Many people are in awe of those with status or those in positions of authority. Even more fascinating is the fact that there are different images that people get extremely attached to. Recall that those who are readily swayed respect individuals in positions of authority. Furthermore, persons in positions of authority are conscious of their capacity to manipulate others by never criticizing them. Rather, they manipulate their ideas and change how they make decisions by employing intricate and deceptive strategies.

enticing to come across

Politicians and other skilled manipulators and scam artists frequently claim to have encountered or experienced particular circumstances, making them individuals in positions of authority. Even when they have limited experience, they can use this appeal to experience to project a picture of someone capable and attack their opponent's lack of experience. This manipulation technique is easy to spot when someone is attempting to exaggerate their knowledge of a specific topic.

Making use of fear

Fears exist in people. The cunning manipulators understand that people will generally react angrily when these feelings of dread are expressed. They then talk to themselves as though they can protect people from these threats, even if they cannot do so. This is similar to what we discussed when we discussed showing the target, without actually giving it to them, how their most wanted outcome is feasible. However, certain lawmakers and politicians regularly employ this strategy to ensure that people support administrative specialists and comply with the demands of the legislature or government authorities.

Making an empathetic plea

To instill frustration in the public with their current circumstances, manipulators can present themselves and their circumstances to the public.

By employing this tactic, the manipulator gains the ability to divert attention from people who could be experiencing a similar situation. However, most politicians would appeal to pity to divert public attention from issues that do not ultimately result in their downfall.

Making use of popular interests

Tricksters and manipulators constantly present themselves to the audience with the appropriate traits and viewpoints, especially about the crowd's revered beliefs. Everyone has biases, and many people disdain some individuals or objects.

Appealing to trust

This strategy is firmly connected with the past points; nevertheless, it accentuates what appears to have breezed through the challenge of time. Social conventions and the norms and traditions of their way of life oppress people regularly. What is commonly accepted as proper tends to seem like the right choice. It is important to remember that manipulators assume that the ideologies and beliefs that the audience is familiar with are sacred. Some assert that their enemy wants to eradicate social norms and practices completely.

Furthermore, they don't worry about whether these customs harm innocent people. From the audience's viewpoint, they appear to be independent, but this is usually the complete opposite. People have realized that people are generally wary of those who defy established norms and societal standards. They are aware enough to avoid these. This leads to a form of limitation on social traditions' unintentional and negligent binding.

Making a fake conflict

It is a real challenge when we have to choose between two equally inappropriate options. When we believe we have two equally inadmissible options out of the many available to us, we face a false dilemma. Consider the argument that goes with it: "We should give up some of our traditional freedoms and rights, or we will lose the war on terrorism."

People are usually ready to admit they are in a fake issue because not everyone agrees with the intricate requirements. Their deceptive strategies include clearing absolutes. Decisions must be fundamental and unambiguous.

Taking a stance on what you say

It is common for manipulators to retreat behind words, refusing to yield or provide direct responses. This allows them to retreat when things get tough. When they are discovered to be forgetting information important to the current circumstance, they immediately devise an excuse. Ultimately, they might yield if coerced, but if you want to be a great manipulator, you must own up to your errors, hide your misdeeds, and never back down from a position of strength.

The Roots of Manipulation Are Fear and Unworthiness

What drives someone to use manipulative strategies to confirm a perfect motive?

The primary explanation—fear—is self-explanatory!

Fears include: what will happen to my life if I don't start this, and will someone else take advantage of me in the future?; that life and others won't give well; that life and others are positioned against this individual; that others would get what they want; and that there are limited assets in a "no-nonsense" world that need to be verified and controlled to endure inwardly, essentially, or monetarily.

Right now, how about we dig a little bit more?

The anxiety beneath the manipulating displays stems from a person's perceived lack of worth.

This can be interpreted as "I am not worthy of life working out for me" or "I am not worthy of life because others are benefiting from my life in the long run on a fundamental level."

An individual's self-perception is essentially shaped by how they perceive themselves about others and life.

Thus, I sincerely believe that I am dishonorable to get better.

Lack of Consciousness Is The Basis Of Manipulation

When we cannot recognize that we are responsible for our reality, we are said to be lacking consciousness. Ignorance is the inability to see the direct connection between events in one's life and one's inner state of being.

This link suggests that it doesn't matter what someone consciously brings to the world because the true indicator of where their awareness lies and what will ultimately unfold is the passionate goal beneath that introduction.

The frameworks of so inside and so without are unbeatable.

Ignorant individuals refuse to acknowledge the existence of this framework despite the repeated instances, agonizing scenarios, and disheartening disappointments. This is what inner feelings and the outside world express when they don't learn from previous experiences.

This is the stagnation state.

Ignorant people accept that manipulation is the greatest way to achieve results in an apparently "hazardous world," even when these results don't lead to lasting fulfillment and repeatedly land back at the beginning.

At that point, additional manipulation ought to be performed to keep a safe distance from this suffering.

What makes manipulation profitable in addition to the basic "handy solution"? Manipulation is a guarded response meant to counterbalance feelings of humiliation, misery, and terror because it is neither a successful nor authentic activity.

It's a deliberate activity that isn't altered in light of more obvious advantages.

It is unquestionably evident to the point of non-understanding. The individual result is invalid when one seeks to profit through deception rather than sincerity.

Anything gleaned from that level of transparency can only result in hollow victories, never-ending suffering, emptiness, terror, and greater shame.

A desperate withdrawal from life and other people, dishonor is the fear of being ashamed of not being loved and appreciated by others and life itself.

It is an estrangement from unity.

In this sense, the only people at the core of their power are those who feel ashamed.

Narratives that explain how to identify manipulators are very common these days. Hundreds, if not thousands, of pages depicting narcissists and trying to teach you how to see the warning signs and respond appropriately, will come up in a quick web search. These articles, which should come as no surprise, explain how to spot a manipulator, identify them, keep your distance from them, and remember that it's okay. I often feel a profundity about how, while we calmly toss out findings here and names there and attempt to paint the whole picture of evil spirits onto people with a broad brush without any regard for subtlety, we never seem to get to the bottom of what's happening and understanding the circumstance for what it is. This book aims to address this issue and improve the reader's understanding of the manipulator. This book provides a framework for understanding; it does not aim to endorse or condone the actions of manipulators.

I'll own it: I was a manipulator for a good deal of the extended periods of my life. I should add that I had no idea what the heck was about to happen. I must confess to you now that I was also an extremely bad one. Therefore, this story comes directly from my perception of what it was like and what I am today. I had to take an intense responsibility to change and put my focus inside. This is my way of taking part of the blame for my own mistakes, providing you with insufficient guidance to help you identify and avoid manipulators, and, maybe, offering some helpful advice that will demonstrate how to behave in a way that will lessen conflict and chaos.

When they're upset and just want to be ignored, a manipulative person may claim they need attention. At that time, they may appear completely fed up with you and even harassed. They could overlook important details in a story, hoping you won't understand them and painting you as the enemy. Regretfully, they might even persuade you that you were incorrect. Have you experienced this or anything similar? Manipulation is what this is.

How to Spot Persuasion Techniques and Determine Whether Someone Is Trying to Trick Us

The subject of persuasion is fascinating. Many persuasive techniques are seen as acceptable in society. They are acceptable; some people even work where persuasion is a major part of their duties. Persuasion is any effort made by one person to get another person to do something. A car dealership salesperson persuades a customer to buy a new car. This isn't thought to be evil or nasty. The distinction is that both sides gain from this persuasion and other instances of a similar nature. The "victim" receives a new car, and the car dealer gets a sale and some money.

Many acceptable forms of persuasion exist that aren't associated with dark psychology. The car above dealer scenario is a common one. It is an effective type of persuasion when a negotiator uses their abilities to convince a terrorist to release their hostage. Persuasion is effective when you can get someone to attend an event they will find enjoyable. Positive persuasion is the term for this kind of persuasion. Then again, what would be considered "dark persuasion"?

Comprehending Shadowy Persuasion

The motivation behind persuasion is the first distinction between dark and good persuasion that you will notice. Positive persuasion is employed when trying to convince someone to do something that won't hurt them. In some circumstances, such as when the negotiator saves a hostage, this persuasion can help save lives.

But there isn't a moral motivation when it comes to dark persuasion. The motivation is frequently immoral and typically amoral. Dark persuasion is more of an attempt to get people to act against their interests if positive persuasion is seen as a means of assisting them in helping themselves. Sometimes, even understanding that they are probably not making the best decision, people will grudgingly carry out these acts because they are desperate to end the constant attempts at persuasion. In other situations, the most skilled dark persuader will convince their victim that they made a great decision, even when, in reality, the victim is acting contrary to what they intended.

What drives someone who uses dark persuasive techniques, then? The circumstances and the person performing the persuading will determine this. To further their agendas, some people enjoy manipulating and convincing their victims.

Some people will take action with the sole purpose of hurting the other person. Sometimes, the motivation behind a persuader's darkly persuasive tactics is to hurt the other person rather than to gain anything from deceiving their target. Nevertheless, others relish the power this form of persuasion grants them.

Additionally, you'll discover that the results of dark persuasion are not the same as positive persuasion. One of three outcomes will result from positive persuasion, including the following:

The one under persuasion gains from this.

Both the persuaded and the persuader stand to gain from this.

A third party and the persuaded party both stand to gain from this.

Since the individual being convinced will benefit from all of these outcomes, they are all desirable.

Other people may occasionally gain from these deeds. However, the party that has been persuaded will always win in all three scenarios.

The result of using dark persuasion will be very different. When someone uses their desire for power or influence, they are the ones who will always come out on top. When someone is being convinced, they frequently listen against their better judgment and do not stand to gain from this deceptive reasoning.

The most adept dark persuaders can also hurt others in the process, in addition to being able to hurt their victims to some extent while simultaneously benefiting themselves.

Revealing The Shadowy Convictor

You might be wondering now who is employing these dubious techniques of persuasion. Is there somebody who would genuinely be interested in using this form of persuasion to damage others?

A dark persuader's primary traits are either a lack of concern or indifference to persuasion's effects on other people. Individuals who employ this type of persuasion are frequently egocentric and prioritize their demands over those of others.

They might even be psychopathic and incapable of understanding the feelings of others.

This form of devious persuasion will frequently manifest itself in a relationship. Usually, one spouse, but occasionally both, will try dark persuasion on the other. This kind of connection will be categorized as psychological abuse if these attempts are sustained and continuous, which is unhealthy for the victim. Until it's too late and they are trapped there, they frequently won't recognize that anything is wrong or that they are being duped.

Examples of this type of dark persuasion in relationships abound. Dark persuasion may occur when one partner prevents the other from accepting a new job offer or forbids them from going out with friends. The dark persuader's strategy aims to persuade the victim that their actions benefit the relationship. The victim is going through a process that is detrimental to both the relationship and themselves.

The Skill of Writing Powerful Lies

There is a huge difference between marketing a falsehood and just telling one. When a preschooler tells a falsehood about who painted the living room wall, everyone can tell. But how do you craft a convincing and convincing story when it comes time to practice deception?

A falsehood must have some basis in reality to be persuasive. It will be simpler to recall, and if you are discovered, you may argue that you merely embellished the facts rather than lying outright. Additionally, you should simplify your lie as much as possible to reduce the number of details that could go wrong. Practice your deceit if you have time to prepare it. It will flow much more easily when it's time to share it.

It is best not to involve anyone else in your falsehoods since the more people are aware of your deception, the more likely it is that you will be discovered. It's preferable to keep secrets and lies to yourself. When telling your falsehood, you should speak naturally and concisely. Ensure your words and body language are consistent and that you can persuade yourself of what you're trying to express.

After you have lied, dispose of any supporting documentation. Delete any social media posts you made. Make sure you throw away any paper you may have written something on. Above all, avoid compounding your lies by telling additional lies. It might be preferable to just admit if you are discovered. Why? Because you're less likely to be caught the next time if you're honest and upfront.

Pants on Fire

If you could catch someone lying because their pants caught fire, wouldn't that be amazing? Sadly, the phrase "liar, liar, pants on fire" isn't true. There are ways to detect when someone is lying without using flames. When someone speaks to you, pay attention to their eyes. If they are easily distracted or appear unable to maintain eye contact, they could not be telling the truth.

But being able to lie involves more than just shifty eyes and fidgeting. Someone can lie to you if they exhibit a behavioral pause or speech delay that they don't usually display. According to some experts, touching one's face or throat while speaking—or playing with or running one's fingers through one's hair—is a dead giveaway that someone is lying.

Speech cues may also serve as indicators of dishonesty. Before responding, if someone asks you the same question twice, they can be buying time to prepare a fake response. If someone asks you a straight question, you should also be aware of ambiguity or lack of information. Ask the person to repeat their tale to you in reverse if you think they are lying to you. If they have to speak a falsehood out of order, they can make a mistake due to the cognitive load of remembering it.

Although there is no infallible method to tell if someone is lying to you, you can increase your odds of seeing deceit by using these suggestions and following your instincts. Never undervalue your instincts; they are far more insightful than speech patterns or body language.

Fundamental Ideas in Persuasion

The fundamental ideas of persuasion are as follows:

An audience is required.

Whether speaking to a huge gathering of people or just one person, persuasion and influence requires listeners. It is imperative that you develop the ability to swiftly adapt to your listener's needs, wants, fears, and desires because this element of persuasion cannot be ignored or modified. You must become an expert in the science of audience reading and background research if you hope to ensure your success.

You must also understand the precise methods and instruments that need to be applied in each circumstance. This is because using poor or improper methods and resources will only obstruct communication with your audience, thus decreasing the likelihood that you will persuade them.

The Capacity to Persuade Is an Equitable Strength

You must comprehend the concept of neutrality to fully grasp the art of persuasion. Remember that persuasion has neither good nor evil rules or skills. The ability to influence others can develop cooperation or compel submission, much as nuclear technology, which can be used to construct an atomic weapon or generate electricity. Whether or not these concepts are applied positively or negatively depends on the person using them and how he applies them.

Some people will stop at nothing to get success. They are prepared to misuse the persuasion principles and employ every trick in the book. To obtain what they desire, they also frequently resort to violence, seduction, bribery, blackmail, and guilds.

However, when applied correctly, persuasion can support the development of a community. We can use persuasion to start fund-raising campaigns, broker peace agreements between warring nations, and persuade motorists to abide by traffic laws.

securing

When mastered, this approach is a potent means of persuasion that may be applied to many contexts. By contrasting two goods, you can convince someone to agree with you by giving them the impression that they are receiving a better deal. This is a persuasive strategy that salespeople frequently employ.

For instance, you visit a car lot and observe a vehicle that costs $12,000.00. You convince the salesman to settle for $9,500, thinking you've struck gold. The car is worth $8,000; therefore, the dealership made money. You feel that the deal went well because they agreed to your negotiated price. The salesperson convinced you that the price you paid was reasonable.

Adaptation Is Needed for Persuasion

It's not enough to copy other people's persuasive techniques to become effective. You must have a solid plan to apply to the various scenarios you encounter. Furthermore, you shouldn't just commit every tactic to memory.

You must actively watch, consider, study, and practice appropriate persuasion concepts if you want to master this ability.

Effective Persuasion Has Durable Impacts

Persuasion that works is fantastic because it leaves a lasting impression, but it requires careful planning and a strong commitment from the speaker. You must invest time and energy to ensure that your remarks have a lasting impact.

Short-term persuasive techniques might appear perfect because they don't take much work, but in the long run, you'll waste more time and energy because your audience will quickly forget what you said.

Ultimately, you must repeat the same procedure to convince your audience to accept what you are saying.

Social Evidence

Consensus is another name for this essential persuasive technique. Narratives of dedication and reliability directly nourish social evidence. We have a narrative that we have told ourselves about who we think we are, what we stand for, and how we behave. We use other people's actions as social proof of how individuals like us ought to respond in specific circumstances to support that narrative.

Power

The next phase is to look for competent people to confirm what we have convinced ourselves is true once we have determined what kind of person we are and have gathered with people who we feel support that identity. That is the point at which authority is established.

Using the pronoun "we,"

Making others feel like they are not alone is crucial to persuasiveness. Never use "you" when speaking to someone to persuade them; rather, use "we." They will believe that by following your instructions, they are also benefiting themselves. In addition, it gives them a sense of belonging, which is a powerful incentive to do something against their better judgment.

Limited availability

About the early stages of evolution, it is evident that our last persuasive concept originated from the earliest stages of survival. We place a higher value on scarcity, so when something appears to be in limited supply, we are more likely to want it.

Because human survival depends on certain resources, which can occasionally be scarce, people are predisposed to try to keep and hold onto things that aren't always available. We will see that this is a common persuasion technique in today's world since it is fundamental to how our minds are wired.

ADVANTAGES THAT NEURO-LINGUISTIC PROGRAMMING MAY OFFER

Behavioral modification techniques such as neurolinguistic programming, or NLP, are employed by psychologists, physicians, hypnotists, and general counselors. Since its invention and introduction in the 1970s, neurolinguistic programming has been a well-liked supplementary tool for bringing about good personal transformation.

A psychological method of communication and self-improvement, neurolinguistic programming focuses on the connection between language and the mind and how it influences our body and behavior. This also involves using targeted visualizations in conjunction with particular linguistic practices to encourage positive transformation from within. NLP results have been all over the place for years; they have included things like decreased anxiety, better memory and focus, weight loss, and the ability to spot deception. These claims have been successfully supported by a few tests, suggesting that NLP could be a useful supplemental treatment for certain people.

1. encourages weight loss

Their mental states may influence the eaters' eating patterns more than their hunger. As such, psychological and behavioral change can assist in reducing an individual's food intake and increase their exercise frequency. According to one study, even if they struggled to maintain their exercise regimen, those aiming to lose weight discovered that participating in NLP had positive effects.

2. It promotes understanding

Training can be difficult, so giving up will make it even more difficult. According to one study, NLP can help children with dyslexia feel more confident in themselves, which may impact their ability to learn. Experts conclude that more research is necessary, especially for people with ADD/ADHD.

3. aid in lowering anxiety
Not surprisingly, NLP provides this advantage as talking and other therapeutic modalities are particularly successful in managing anxiety. A study analyzing individuals who had claustrophobia as a result of MRI scans revealed that NLP was a very successful technique for reducing anxiety, and other research supported this finding. It is believed that the combination of focused and relaxing visualization may be the main factor contributing to NLP's ability to reduce anxiety.

4. It encourages emotional balance.
There is insufficient data to conclude that NLP can be a helpful strategy for fostering general emotional well-being. But remember that depression is a result of many personal

characteristics that are specific to each person and that treating depression requires a multimodal strategy that is customized for each person. The total solution may benefit from the application of NLP.

5. aids in overcoming negative habits

Replacing a bad behavior with a new positive habit is one of the most effective strategies to break a bad habit. The NLP was one of the most popular methods for assisting people in doing just that. NLP is a fantastic weapon that everyone can have in their toolbox to combat unhealthy habits like putting off exercise or overindulging in junk food because it carries no risk of adverse effects.

Techniques in Neuro-Lingual Programming

Adopting another person's customs, attitudes, beliefs, and skills to mimic what they do is called "modeling" in NLP.

1. Meta-method: The meta-method aims to push one's boundaries through a series of targeted questions and language habits. When someone talks about a situation or subject, their terminology—frequently identified as markers in NLP—can change, distort, omit details, and generalize perceptions. The person providing care for the patient will start identifying the problems concealed in the words by listening to and responding to these various linguistic patterns. It is hoped that a therapist who treats the counselor according to the therapist's beliefs and converses with them will miss crucial conversation details and be less equipped to assist the patient appropriately. The Meta-model is designed to swiftly detect negative thought patterns and limit convictions, drawing inspiration from the language practices of Fritz Perls and Virginia Satir. The Meta-Model's questions are intended to help illuminate the patient's underlying

beliefs and cognitive patterns while providing further context for their terminology.

By inquiring about the crucial aspects that have been omitted, the meta-model can be utilized in a business context to assist the client in elaborating and providing more specifics about their goals, proposals, and issues. To begin with, if someone says, "We need to make a decision," the first step in responding to such a statement might be to inquire who will make the decision and how it will be made. Why? Why? The term "decision" alludes to a process that has been converted into an abstract noun and is not identified, but the word "we" does not specify who does the activity.

2. The Milton technique is a type of hypnosis founded on the hypnotist Milton Erickson's hypnotic communication patterns. The Milton procedure consists of three parts. Secondly, to overpower and disorient the conscious mind to

induce involuntary interaction. Second, to support developing and maintaining a patient/client relationship. Second, make sure the patient or client understands the terminology used.

Section Five

NLP Methods

T

The discovered NLP techniques have the potential to drastically alter your perception of reality. Since our thoughts and feelings create our reality, these NLP techniques can alter you for as long as you can remember.

Here are five best NLP systems to help you transform your behavior and project a better future.

NLP Methods That Will Revolutionize Your Life

Divorce

Have you ever found yourself in a situation where you have terrible instincts? Maybe you've come across something that makes you feel depressed every time you come across it. Conversely, you may have anxiety in situations at work where you have to communicate honestly. Maybe when you have to approach that "unique somebody" you've had your eye on, you get shy. Even though these feelings of guilt, fear, or timidity seem to be preprogrammed or uncontrollable, NLP techniques for dissociation can be extremely beneficial.

Determine the emotion you must let go of, such as fear, anger, anxiety, or disgust at the situation.

Envision being able to glide out of your body and look back at yourself, taking in the entire situation as an observer.

Observe how the inclination drastically shifts.

Imagine you can skim out of your body and see yourself to gain even more elevation. Then, coast out of this body again so that you are looking at yourself. Almost every small situation should feel less negative after this two-fold distancing.

Reframing Content

Try using this tactic when you believe that something is unfavorable or helpless. Any bad situation can be made more engaging for you by reframing it such that the experience has a positive meaning.

Assume, for example, that your relationship ends. On the surface, that could seem horrifying, but let's reframe it. What possible benefits might be a single offer? For example, you're open to making new connections right now. You also have the freedom to take care of yourself when necessary. Furthermore, you have gained valuable experience from this relationship that will enable you to make far better connections in the future.

These are all examples of rephrasing a situation. You give yourself a different experience of the separation by reinterpreting its meaning.

It's usual to go into a frenzy or focus on fear when faced with anticipated conditions, but this just causes more problems. It's interesting how shifting your focus to what was just described helps you clear your mind and make deliberate, unbiased decisions.

Protecting Yourself

Securing began with Russian scientist Ivan Pavlov, who experimented with hounds by repeatedly ringing a bell while the dogs were eating. He learned that he could make the dogs salivate by ringing the chime repeatedly, even in the absence of food, after having repeated rings of the device.

This established a neural connection between the ringer and the salivary behavior known as an adapted reaction. These kinds of "grapples" for upgrade reactions are something you can use yourself!

Being confident in oneself pushes you to associate each ideal, passionate, positive response with a particular phrase or feeling. When you intentionally link a positive idea or sensation to a clear signal, you can initiate this grapple anytime you're experiencing a low mood, and your feelings will quickly shift.

Determine your required emotions (assurance, satisfaction, calmness, etc.).

Choose a location on your body where the stay would be useful, such as tearing the cartilage in your ears, coming into contact with a knuckle, or crushing a fingernail. You can effortlessly activate the favorable tendency with this physical contact. Where you choose is irrelevant as long as it is a unique touch you don't contact for any other reason.

Consider a time when you experienced that feeling (certainty, for example). See through your own eyes and recollect that memory as you mentally travel back to that period and float back into your body. Adjust your nonverbal cues to synchronize the state with the memories. As you reflect on those memories, see what you saw, hear what you heard, and experience the need. You'll begin to experience that state. It's similar to telling a fun story to a friend from the past; once you "get into" the story, you start laughing again because you've "partnered" with the story and "remembered" it.

Once you're back in the memory, touch, pull, or press the selected body area. The inclination will increase as you recollect the experience. Release the touch as soon as the intense emotion peaks and fades.

When you make that contact again, a neurological upgrading reaction will initiate the condition. Make the same kind of interaction with yourself again to experience that state (e.g., Confidence).

Consider another recollection in which you experienced that feeling, go back and recall it with your own eyes, and confront the state at the same location as previously to ground the response significantly. Incorporating more memories makes the stay more potent and will elicit a more grounded response.

Establishing And Changing Patterns

Another set of standards used in neuro-linguistic programming is to improve goal formulation and achievement. Some of the most well-known ones can be distinguished, allowing us to apply the approach to our activities and motivations once we've mastered it. Examine your mental map and use it precisely to accomplish your objectives.

And where should you begin your goal-chasing? First, by outlining the course of action and creating the desired outcomes. You cannot move on to the next phase without completing this first step. By visualizing the precise form of your objective, you can anticipate a great deal of information and duties that you might otherwise overlook. For this reason, setting and planning goals can help you progress more quickly and reach your objectives as soon as feasible. You can develop the ability to design your intentions, the desire to make adjustments, and the readiness to work.

It's best to formulate your objectives in affirmative statements, such as "I want to take better care of myself and be in better shape" instead of "I don't want to be fat." The second phrase stimulates thoughts we would like not to think about, which has a paradoxical effect. That tune that "didn't want to leave your head" must have been yours. You can give the objective more strength at this point in its formation, mostly so we have the will and motivation to see it through to completion. Breaking down your objective into manageable chunks is worthwhile, so let's get started. Declaring "I want to run a kilometer" is simpler than committing to a marathon. That adage, "cut its coat according to its cloth," applies to this situation. We shouldn't set ourselves too high of a goal; instead, we should start with something more manageable to motivate us to keep going and get closer to our ultimate objective. It is also necessary to define a deadline for the aim if not a particular timeframe.

Another example is understanding the other person or trying to fit our interlocutor's world model. By "getting into the position of another person," we can better understand the reasons for other people's conduct. This enables us to modify our communication with them to convey more information and our goal for them. When dealing with others, this pattern is especially helpful. Certain persons are kinaesthetic, sights, or listeners. For speedier and more relevant communication, each group should receive a slightly different message based on the prominent traits.

For instance, visionaries tend to talk rapidly, which makes it easier for visuals to be imagined. As a result, it could be challenging for them to get along with kinaesthetics, who are more aware of experiences after they have had personal experience with something. For instance, listeners pay close attention to a speaker's voice and speaking intensity; a calmer, more balanced voice is frequently heard. Frequently, we can reach a consensus faster if we adapt to your interlocutor's traits. It is more important to match messages so that communication is more accurate and flowing without interruptions than pretending to be someone else.

The "state calibration" is another illustration of a pattern in neuro-linguistic programming. It is, in essence, about the senses and their ability to focus. It is the perception and amplification of your interlocutor's feelings and experiences. A great deal of focus on the recipient is necessary. For instance, Bandler and Grinder found that an individual's eye orientation can be linked to a certain mental function of the brain at a particular time. This information aids in our understanding of the other person. For instance, the right-handed person's eye movements to the left and up could represent scenes, to the left and side, sounds, down and left, feelings, and up and right, the interlocutor's visualizations. On the other side, this is how people perceive left-handed people. For instance, you can assess your interlocutor's thoughts, agreement with your viewpoint, and response to discussing a specific problem or subject.

The second pattern, the ecology of the pattern and its verification focuses on confirming the notion of ecology about the mind and body. It asks whether the objectives are equal and whether they consider your feelings towards the particular goal and the environment's demands and psychology's demands. You can accurately ascertain whether your goals, your belief system, and the equilibrium of the mind-body system align. Given the interconnectedness of the body, mind, and emotions, they should cooperate rather than inhibit one another's progress toward the objective. This is how you persistently work toward your objective.

Additionally, you can experiment with a pattern related to the reaction's flexibility because the content of our messages is through particular reactions, regardless of our aims. You already have the power to shape and emulate your responses. We can all benefit from flexibility, a highly helpful quality, particularly in interpersonal connections.

To obtain the desired responses, you can also alter the pattern. Since everyone is unique, communication is facilitated by flexibility or the attempt to fit in with the interlocutor's style. It's important to try to understand people and come to a consensus, even though there may be moments when our opinions disagree with theirs. Everybody wants to elicit certain emotions during the call. As we just discussed, enlargable and amplified visuals are crucial. You can pay attention to your feelings and deliberately feel them. Then, you can choose which emotions to let go or lessen so they don't trigger unhelpful, strong mental states.

Mix and match any pattern to find the best one for you. You will eventually be able to create the states you need more rapidly, as completing all of the exercises will make it easier and easier. It's also important to discuss how to break through the emotional and mental barriers that prevent us from moving forward and force us to halt. For instance, a historical event might also be altered by altering its conclusion or certain details to lessen its influence. Every one of us has undoubtedly experienced circumstances that elicited unfavorable feelings; however, the most crucial thing is to create a network of recollections and positive feelings to stifle those unpleasant feelings. Neuro-linguistic programming helps to mold the future so that our objectives become an alluring vision to realize, the past so that it sustains us, and the present so that we may intentionally trigger the emotional states that drive us at a given moment.

Chapter 3: Practitioners of Mind Control Methods

While some people utilize mind control techniques for selfish purposes, other types of people do it with good motives. When a therapist or counselor tries to use control techniques to help a client overcome addiction, they mean well. However, narcissists, sociopaths, and psychopaths use these strategies for their self-interest. In actuality, these manipulators can use mind control methods only by nature. Such people have no conscience, which allows them to mind control others without considering the repercussions.

Since most people are unaware of the precise definitions of narcissists and psychopaths, manipulators are frequently referred to by other names, such as controlling spouses, controlling husbands, control freak bosses, jealous boyfriends, verbally abusive spouses, or extremely strict managers. Individuals may be suffering from a personality disorder.

victims of mind control

Anybody can fall prey to mind control tactics. Since you are also prone to mind control, you must be able to spot manipulators and end them quickly. There is a fallacy that claims mind control only affects the weak and helpless. Additionally, some individuals think that those who fall prey to mind control are flawed. That is untrue, and I think it is fiction.

Anyone can become a victim of a manipulator; in fact, the more likely someone is to fall into that trap, the more likely they will not be alert.

Knowing the tricks and strategies employed by those who prey on you to draw them in and keep them there is the best defense against mind control and manipulation. Here are a few actual mind control methods employed historically by individuals and organizations and which manipulators continue to utilize today.

Separation

Over the years, various manipulative individuals and groups have utilized isolation as a means to enable abuse. Social, emotional, and physical isolation can have devastating effects. Research indicates that the most effective kind of isolation is physical, but in situations when this isn't possible, the manipulator tries to separate the victim psychologically. Isolation can be accomplished in a variety of methods, including removing the victim from their environment for an extended length of time or casting doubt on the individuals they trust. Restricting the flow of information is one way a manipulator employing mind control on a victim might control any source that could sway the victim.

Remarks

A manipulator will constantly take care to make sure they don't notice anything unusual. As such, he or she will converse with the victim as though they are members of the same team. The victim will feel exalted to be linked with someone with a different perspective on the world because the conversations will mostly centeraround "us against the world." The victim is isolated using this technique.

Social proof and peer pressure

Those who want to control big crowds of people typically employ this tactic. One tactic used to persuade people to believe what others do is social proof. Because "everyone does that," it is right and justifiable, according to the psychological phenomena. This method of mental control is effective when the victims are unsure of what to think or do in a given circumstance. Many people copy the actions of others after observing what they do. Most of us succumb to peer pressure because we don't want to be the oddballs.

Fear of being cut off

A manipulator makes sure the victim depends too much on them. As a result, the sufferer has anxiety about alienation. A person can become blinded by the comforting sense of having someone back them. Furthermore, the deceived individual may be scared to leave even after realizing something is amiss. It may appear dangerous and lonely outside.

Recurrence

Even though manipulation is a common practice used by many people worldwide, it may be a very effective instrument for manipulation. Repetition is a powerful tool for persuasion. Repetition is too easy, when you think about it, to be a powerful, persuasive technique. How is it possible to subdue someone with repeated words and deeds? Nonetheless, if a message is repeated, it becomes easier and more recognizable, which helps it stick in your memory. A person has a good probability of successfully controlling their thoughts if they combine social proof with repetition.

Affirmations are another type of repetition that demonstrates the effectiveness of the method. It is often suggested to those looking for change to continually affirm who they are. People receiving anger management therapy, for example, are encouraged to use statements like

"I can control this anger." I'm in charge of helping them chill down for the moment. Amazingly, these repetitions do the trick; eventually, the person starts to think and act in a particular way.

Weary

An individual's ability to think is hampered by fatigue. You are less attentive when you are fatigued both emotionally and physically. This could allow a manipulator to get in the way of your choices. One study found that, in contrast to those who had enough sleep, those who were sleep-deprived for longer than 21 hours were more prone to believe suggestions, according to the Journal of Experimental Psychology.

establishing a new self

A manipulator's initial move is to reshape your identity so that you follow their instructions. A manipulator's ultimate goal is for you to resemble a puppet or robot—someone who blindly obeys commands. The manipulator will attempt to get you to confess or acknowledge that they are a decent person and that you believe them by using the methods listed above as well as additional mind control techniques.

These con artists won't try to take all of your rights away from you at once. Initially, it will be anything as basic as acknowledging that the manipulator is a decent and motivating individual. It gets simpler to accept things one after the other once you recognize their goodness. Before you know it, you start to sing to the tune of the manipulator because of the way you accept things repeatedly.

What Is the Conjecture?

An assumption formed in light of certain facts is called a hypothesis. Any inquiry that converts research questions into forecasts begins with this. Variables, populations, and the interactions between variables are some of its constituent parts. A hypothesis used to investigate the relationship between two or more variables is known as a research hypothesis.

Potential Features

The qualities of the theory are as follows:

The hypothesis should be clear and correct to make it reliable.

The hypothesis should explain the relationship between the variables if it is relational.

The hypothesis needs to be clear and allow for more testing.

The hypothesis needs to be explained simply, and it should be realized that its simplicity has nothing to do with its significance.

Speculative Source

The potential sources are as follows:

The phenomena are comparable to one another.

Insights from competitors, recent experience, and previous studies.

Theory based on science.

A broad pattern that affects people's cognitive processes.

Imaginary Type

Basic Theory

It illustrates how an independent variable and a dependent variable are related. For instance, you will lose weight more quickly if you consume more vegetables. In this case, weight loss is the dependent variable, and eating more veggies is the independent variable.

Intricate Theory

It illustrates how two or more independent and two dependent variables are related.

Directional Theory

It demonstrates the expertise and dedication of researchers to achieving particular goals. Variables' qualities can also be predicted by their relationship. A four-year-old child's IQ is higher than a child who hasn't eaten anything within the last five years, for instance, if they eat appropriate food. This illustrates the impact and its direction.

Unfocused Hypothesis

When there is no theory involved, it is used. This indicates a relationship between the two variables, but it does not specify the precise type or direction of that relationship.

The null hypothesis

It offers claims that defy presumptions. "HO" is the representation of this sign.

Connection and Causal Theory

The causality hypothesis puts forth the idea of a causal relationship between two or more variables.

Imaginary Example

Based on their classification, the following assumptions are examples:

Regularly consuming sugar-filled beverages can result in obesity. This is a straightforward case study.

A sample of the null hypothesis would be all lilies with an equal number of petals.

A person's level of exhaustion will decrease after 7 hours of sleep as opposed to none at all.

You Can't Measure Hypnosis

Hypnosis is unique because it is nearly impossible to "measure" in any conventional sense. Their brain wave patterns have nothing to do with the typically calm alpha brain waves if their brain wave patterns are seen with EEG equipment. They are not theta waves that are observed in sleep. While some observable indications, like those mentioned above, may emerge during hypnosis, there are no signs that can be measured scientifically. And for this reason, hypnosis is the subject of so much debate. There's no denying its existence when you witness it like we do.

State of Hypnotic "Trance"

Hypnosis can have many tags, and many people choose "to describe this experience. I think it is worth closing this article by discussing its suitability as a description of hypnosis because I don't like the word "like." I prefer to use phrases like hypnosis and relaxation or use hypnosis when possible. However, this is not always possible due to context, so you may be on our website, and one of our articles (including this one) sees "psychedelics." In my opinion, the meaning of "tr" is exactly what many people think of hypnosis over the years—a state of translucent staring. One has no idea what is happening around them and is completely powerless. Talk about loopholes! No wonder many people are full of doubts and fears about the whole process of hypnosis until they discover the true meaning! Many people never Discover the true meaning of hypnotism because they are so convinced of what will happen or may happen to them that they will never have the opportunity to find opportunities for themselves. For these people, the urban myths about hypnosis hang over those "People who are in trouble" or "go too far to grow up again." They hear or imagine they hear someone "turned into a zombie" or watch a movie in which someone is turned into a fearless murderer, Machines, or the same weird things. These kinds of stories abound. Paradoxically, their fear-hypnosis is the only thing that causes them to "indulge" in these stories! And those who have such views have already been captured. Hypnosis is hypnotized. Hypnosis is particularly focused on an idea or concept, as was previously said. Alright, that's it. Only a ton of creativity and total focus may start to make it plausible, even real; there is no logic.

Dark Psychology: Who Uses It To Impact People?

You may be thinking that since you don't want to dominate people, you don't need to learn dark psychology. Even though this may be the case, understanding dark psychology is crucial. Dark psychology is not something we study to gain power over others. The only reason we study dark psychology is to defend ourselves against people who are skilled at manipulation. You will come across dark folks even if you do not study dark psychology. Even though everyone is somewhat bad, humans have extremely high degrees of evil in their systems. Some people are constantly on the lookout for someone else to harm. It would be better to shield oneself from those people by figuring out their motivations and thoughts before they ever speak with you. Several social groupings profit greatly by manipulating others through the use of dark psychology. You must defend yourselves against them. Among those who apply dark psychology are politicians, love partners, and coworkers.

Rivals of The Workplace: You may think that only certain individuals employ dark psychology methods. It's a fact that everyone is dark. If you were at all perceptive, you would have realized that even your mother could manipulate your life with dark psychology. The workplace is one of the most frequent locations for dark psychology. This is as a result of a drive for achievement. Power in the job since everyone wants to succeed in whatever they do. You must exercise extreme caution if you are in a high position at work. Dark psychologists typically target positions of authority. Dark psychologists are aware that they may have a compelling motive to take control of your life if they can infiltrate your mind and obtain information using methods like nonverbal communication (NLP). One thing to get better at is keeping any information about your desires private. You can suffer at the hands of manipulators if you cannot conceal any pertinent aspects of your personality.

Political Leaders: Politicians are among the people who also employ dark psychology. Politicians will go to any lengths to increase their influence and authority. Being influential is one of the main goals of dark psychology. People will work to increase their influence and authority if they wish to rule your life. Political leaders use dark psychology tactics like brainwashing and persuasion to master the art of mass control. They can turn your weaknesses against you once they discover them. They manipulate the electorate and employ dark psychology to undermine their rivals.

Managing Relationship Partners: Another subset of those who profit greatly from the application of dark psychology is that of managing partners. Some people are only at ease when in charge of their relationships. They put a lot of effort into making sure they are in control of the relationship. These individuals will stop at nothing to maintain total control over the relationship. Making decisions is not granted to you by a domineering relationship partner. They'll employ NLP tactics to get insight into your personality and then apply those strategies to manipulate your behavior. It is simple for someone to take control of your life if they can learn and become an expert in your ways. NLP is a tool that dark psychologists use to log your ideas. They leverage your understanding of how you live and conduct business.

Workplace Modifiers. Identify and Dispose of Them

Having an impact: Three types of appeals can be used to classify tactics: cooperative, logical, and passionate. Put more simply, it affects the hands, heart, or head.

Appealing to people's logic and intellect is known as logical Appeal. In this category, you will make an appealing case for the optimal course of action based on organizational or individual benefits.

Emotional Appeal: this relates your initiative, message, or objective to personal objectives and values. This can be done by creating concepts that appeal to one's sense of service, well-being, or belonging. If this works, there's a good possibility the rest of the team will support it, which is much needed.

Cooperative Appeals translates to "collaboration," therefore, what are the tasks you will accomplish jointly? While consultation entails hearing other people's opinions, it's crucial to form coalitions with people who have previously supported you or provided much-needed legitimacy. That is why working together in an organization toward a single goal may be quite beneficial. Reaching out to people can be a useful strategy for persuasion. It should be noted that leaders adept at using these persuasion techniques can accomplish their aims and objectives in any setting—including organizations—with greater success. Regardless of their managerial roles within the company, we cannot say the same about leaders who lack these abilities.

Which Persuasion Strategy Is Best for You? When selecting the impact that will be most beneficial to you, take into account the following strategies:

Recognize Your Readership. Determine who your stakeholders are and what they believe. This is because everyone has their agenda, worries, priorities, and points of view. Furthermore, various individuals and groups will require various persuading techniques. It will be crucial to adapt your persuading strategy to each individual. Keeping in mind each person's unique characteristics, aspirations, and goals, as well as the roles and duties within the business.

Evaluate the circumstances. You should start by asking yourself some basic questions, like: Why am I involved in this field? Why do I need the opinion of this other person? What kind of outcomes do I hope to accomplish by influencing this individual? In this category, being blatantly explicit about who you need to influence and your goals is one of the most crucial things to remember. Review Your Ability. Which strategies do you occasionally employ? Which ones work best when applied? Are there any novel strategies that could be applied here? Can you also draw inspiration or guidance from others? Let's say, for instance, that you are constantly focused on persuading colleagues with reason. If that's the case, it's wise to have a highly committed collaborator on your team to support your collaboration strategies and arguments.

Think Through Your Strategy. Which strategies are the most effective for you? Which logical arguments, in your opinion, work best when applied? How can you appeal to someone's emotions or their cooperation? In each strategy, how would you specifically phrase or act? You must consider potential answers to ensure that you have sufficiently prepared your response. Do you have any refutations you could make? Are there any other strategies to help you influence others?

It is imperative that, while beginning a career in leadership or management, you practice one-on-one and experiment with new influencing strategies in low-risk settings. You will become enough confident in your talents to influence other teams and larger groups as you become more adaptable and experienced. You will gain confidence in persuading people in high-pressure circumstances due to this experience. Choose the strategy that suits you the most.

www.ingramcontent.com/pod-product-compliance
Lightning Source LLC
Chambersburg PA
CBHW052151110526
44591CB00012B/1932